THE BRUISE
OF YOUR ABSENCE

poems by

Cris Mulvey

Finishing Line Press
Georgetown, Kentucky

THE BRUISE
OF YOUR ABSENCE

Copyright © 2020 by Cris Mulvey
ISBN 978-1-64662-304-4 First Edition
All rights reserved under International and Pan-American Copyright Conventions. No part of this book may be reproduced in any manner whatsoever without written permission from the publisher, except in the case of brief quotations embodied in critical articles and reviews.

ACKNOWLEDGMENTS

"Ceremony" (P. 19) in *Echoes Journal*, Issue 13, Fall-Winter 2011, and *Echoes Anthology*, Issue 14, Fall-Winter 2012.
"Last Time" (P. 20) as "Last Cuppa" in *Naugatuck River Review*, Issue 18, Aug. 2017.

Publisher: Leah Maines
Editor: Christen Kincaid
Cover Art: Cris Mulvey
Author Photo: Jack Kuehn
Cover Design: Elizabeth Maines McCleavy

Printed in the USA on acid-free paper.
Order online: www.finishinglinepress.com
also available on amazon.com

Author inquiries and mail orders:
Finishing Line Press
P. O. Box 1626
Georgetown, Kentucky 40324
U. S. A.

Table of Contents

Dreaming 1

Early Morning 2

Burning 3

Argument 4

Faithful 5

Waiting 6

Overtaken 7

On My Dead Mother's Birthday 8

The Way That Flowers Can Open You 9

Father 11

Banished 12

Adoption 13

Remembering The Day I Placed My Child 14

My Birth Son Writes Back 15

The Sea Outside My Window Smells Of You 16

After 17

After Hearing Of My Daughter-In-Law's Miscarriage 18

Ceremony 19

Last Time 20

Burial 21

Visiting Your Husband's Grave 22

One A.m And The House Is Quiet 24

Last Moment 25

I Know You Chose To Leave 26

As You Lie Dying Far Away 27

Singing Over The Bones 28

*For my beloved friend Emer,
who left this world on Jan. 20, 2020,
and for all my other loved ones already departed.*

DREAMING

I want to live
where the knots and burls of the open Front
jump to the shell of sky.

There, beneath the massive reefs,
in amongst the stones, I want to see you stamp
your feet, send clouds of blue

into the freezing air;
lug wood, fling it to the brittle ground;
stoke the fire for tea.

I want to watch you read
on and on into the endless night, while northern lights
blow colored smoke across the stars.

I want that sky, filled with wind or snow, I do not care.
I want its spaciousness flung 'round me,
as it's flung around those stones.

I want to be those stones,
staring at the empty skull of sky,
ringing.

EARLY MORNING

Waking in the first pale light of day,
last night's love sounds in my ear.

Outside, the vast white arc of winter.

Now, downstairs, the thud of wood,
clink of grate. Door slammed.

Inside, the vast white arc of silence.

Last night's love sounds
still in my ear.

BURNING

Tonight is a night of fire,
stars spinning to dust,

your pillow beside me,
empty.

Outside, in the moonlight,
snow is falling, ash on stone,

stuff of the dreams that
call you to me.

I want to fall like that,
in drifts upon your skin.

I want to enter in. I want to
gaze into your eyes—my heat unsheathed!

I want you with me.

ARGUMENT

In the rounded portals of your eyes
there is a moving darkness where I long to hide.

I am a branch caught in the trees'
mad clutch, flung there by desire.

I am a solitary shell, filling and emptying
with surf, frothing, winking out,

my yearning turning cold inside me,
like your engine in the night,

too cold to spark,
now roaring into life.

Sweep of headlights as you leave,
red taillights in the midnight snow,

the slow return of silence, washing
over me, waves on the night-cold sand,

black ripples catching the stars.
As soon as you are gone,

I want you.

FAITHFUL

From stone locked strands I watch the trance
of leaves on water, flight of geese between the clouds,
pine needles skittering in the wind.

I wait for you,
fire at my core.
I wait.

Long years from now, they'll find me
here, wind whistling through my ribs, my eyes
two empty moons of longing.

WAITING

On days like this, when the moisture-laden sky
lies like the belly of a fish over the sepia hills, the mossy trees,
the earth is an old, old photograph awaiting color.

On days like this, when the pearl-grey clouds cling,
shapeless as a towel, to the distant hills, the sky moves here amongst us,
fingering the body of the earth with tender curiosity.

In the silence there's a constant hum,
like the distant droning of a car. The world looks inward,
arms wrapped 'round itself, half sleeping, barely breathing.

Again, again, I think I hear you coming.
Like the windless forest, I hold my breath
and for a second hang, like rain un-fallen,

waiting.

OVERTAKEN

Behind this forest cabin I've been renting
since we parted, an abandoned garden: weak
tangle of morning glory knotted through

the thin wire squares of its fence, almost
hiding the twisted tines of a rake. Plastic leis,
pink and yellow, hung on the rusted gate.

Inside, tall stalks of fennel, cracked
pots strewn in the matted lilies, five raised beds
sprouting a fury of weeds.

In the center, one metal chair, its blue paint peeling
onto the ground, and everywhere, the forest
creeping back, its slow shadows stroking the air.

By the broken shed, I catch my image
in a window, and for a moment
I don't know who I am—hair uncombed,

face gone to seed, skin like dried-out dirt—
untended at the end of the day, my time too running out,
so much older than I remember.

ON MY DEAD MOTHER'S BIRTHDAY

Four years since I listened on the phone
to your last out-breath, six thousand miles away.

How often have I searched for you—
through the grizzled mist of mountain,

in the violet pockets of the sea—
green dew of your absence, cold upon my shoulders?

This morning, the grey grate
of my kitchen has no ember.

This single slice of orange
pulses purple on my tongue.

When the crow's cry catches the air,
you are still nowhere to be found.

THE WAY THAT FLOWERS CAN OPEN YOU

On this, what would have been your ninetieth birthday,
I remember your forty-ninth: A summer's day. The three of us
whispering in my room, making you a "bouquet"—

weaving a bruised and dangerous wilderness
of rose and fuschia, daisies, your beloved iris,
into the long, lithe blades of rushes

we had gathered from the tangled ditches
pouring their riotery into the lane
that wandered from our cottage to the sea;

wrapping it in cellophane, diaphanous and wide,
to make it look just like the ones (you said) they give
to ballerinas, in Leningrad or Paris,

places you could never go, though you dreamed
about their avenues of marble, glimmering
in the velvet blues and golds of candlelight and snow.

At twelve, lifting the sheaf to our outstretched arms,
we carried it across the hall,
through the open doorway of the kitchen where you stood,

back to the door, peeling spuds and humming along
to Perry Como on the radio, *Mona Lisa, Mona Lisa*.
Sun from the open window made a halo of your hair.

Your arms shimmered with wet and the tip
of your tongue was rubbing your upper lip,
the way it always did when you were working.

We stood behind you, flowers laid flat across our arms,
the way you laid your ironing on the back of Daddy's chair,
carefully, with precision, so as not to make a crease,

the way you carried them to put them all away,
the way you carried me to hospital that day when I was five,
and stung unconscious, and you thought I might be dead.

"Mammy," we cried, all three of us, our excitement frilling
the air, and you turned to face us, gasping, your grey eyes
filling with tears, arms outstretched for the flowers.

We laid the "bouquet" over them,
the way they must have laid the broken body
of your Jesus over his mother's lap,

the way that later, decades later,
we laid the heavy cream of lilies over
the newly heaped-up earth of your grave.

FATHER

Those were the days when the steel, blue-gray
of the Atlantic moved in your eyes

and you'd go striding the wind-lashed shore,
where cracked rocks walked into wave and ocean,

your lungs heave-gulping the salted air
by the bucketful, to catch the tide.

Or oars in hand, you'd battle hungry seas,
electrified by the purple hulk of cloud and sun,

reading the word of Yahweh from the flight
of one, wild gull whipped to silver by the day's last light.

You were a God that worshipped me,
making magic out of everything you touched.

Time, and time again, I'd watch your hands
close 'round the slippery plumpness of another fish.

Talking, as I wished you'd talk to me, you'd free its hook
and fling it on a fin of rock 'til later, when knives in hand,

we'd slit and gut and clean the squeaky flesh,
smell of its life sharp in our nostrils,

scales of it still on our fingers,
when we slept.

BANISHED

The journey on the boat is uneventful.
What I remember is the train, the shooting fields,
and over them my wan reflection in the window, hovering.

Still unbelieving, my hands laid flat
on the early fullness of my womb, its taut flesh throbbing,
everyone I know, a sea away.

The train tears on, hurtling towards
its strange horizon, where trees spread out their
broken wings. This is a going down.

It must be done alone.

ADOPTION

I.
You, my just-born, dressed in white, I dare not hold you.
I watch your popping-mouthed gaze.

I touch your cheek, put my pinky
in your tiny fist.

I turn away.

Inside, a knife is slicing slabs of flesh, carving
bone. A hole is opening and I am falling.

II.
The car we sit in speeds through country roads,
hedges greening with the first, crisp pricks of Spring.

You're sleeping, body heavy in my arms,
head pressed against my breasts; your eyelids quivering.

I listen to your breath, its soft, sweet clicking,
feel its warmth damp against my hand.

One last time.

III.
At home, after you've been handed over, after dinner,
I climb the stairs to bed, my hollow body thick, a stranger.

In the room, I think there is a mirror,
or maybe it's a cold, blank wall.

I press my cheek against its flatness,
my two hands hanging

empty by my sides.

REMEMBERING THE DAY I PLACED MY CHILD

Just now, a wind moved through this clearing where I sit.
The tall grass swayed, bowed low.

I remember the maw of that summer's day in Dublin,
concrete walls of the suburbs where I lived,

dogs barking in the distance,
my parents watching telly.

Here, I search for forgotten things—old bones
in a ditch, dried blood smeared on a stone,

last night's rain beaded on a see-through
scrap of plastic.

Around me fields of the winged casings
of seeds, already flown—dried out husks,

slivers of silver—leaning empty
into the wind.

MY BIRTH SON WRITES BACK

Back from the river,
its waves of air and slatted shadow, stone-warm

musk of eucalyptus, spackled banks shivering
with birdwing and the filaments of webs silked by sun,

your letter on my floor,
dropped like a pebble into the pool

of my waiting—white feather on the river's back,
skin of its light spinning,

I reach for you, the small wind of my breath
like pine needles skittering.

Blue words scratched on a torn-out sheet,
lure of your smell, fragile as the girl

I buried thirty years ago, when I gave you
to another. Fragile as the tie that binds us now,

the bruise of your absence
opening around me.

THE SEA OUTSIDE MY WINDOW SMELLS OF YOU

This window that's been shut all winter,
this window that today—the day the snow began to quiver
and let down its guard—

this window that I opened just this morning,
your warmth still filling the folds of my body, before I filled the kettle,
made the coffee, gave the dog her breakfast,

before your absence hit…

this window I threw open to the smell of sea,
trees leaping, wet soil sending its tendrils out,
relentlessly pushing into the dark, just like you,

now that you've finally left…

this window where I sit, surrounded by the dark
and thrashing waters of my dreams, color of night skies around the moon,
flared foil, torn waves breaking over the cold,

worn sands of my grieving…

this window, that ocean, my body,
one great longing
for your smell.

AFTER

Through the first sweet light of morning
the oars of my boat are riding like the wings of the red-tails gliding,
high on the thermals over the mountains.

From the still-dark pane of the lake, fog
is pluming, like the last hot breath of the wild deer dying, steaming
the frosted air, wishing nobody harm.

Nothing is the same
now. It is over.

Holding our life together as though
it were a bubble, I watch it glisten, watch it burst,
then disappear. If I could,

I would howl,
like a lone wolf in winter,
after the feast.

AFTER HEARING OF MY DAUGHTER-IN-LAW'S MISCARRIAGE

All week while I cooked, washed dishes, read books
to her child, she talked on her cell, its blue screen lighting
the half open door to her room.

Each word we said, a veiling.

Yesterday, on the beach, her daughter played at my feet,
ramming her bucket with dead things—old kelp, cupped shells,
the rusted claws of crabs. Out on the open ocean,

the wind changed direction.

Today, billions of jellyfish driven to shore,
their tiny, once translucent sails, those blue-rimmed
membranes, dulled and flaking

like dried-out blood, crusting the beach.

Now, standing where this river meets the ocean,
a cold sky filling with cloud, its wild cape
of wind whipping around me, I watch the sea spill

wings of water, over and over, listen to the waves' long sighs,
straining their way back through the gravel
into the vastness, everything I wish I'd said,

sand in the wind's flung fist.

CEREMONY

In our circle,
there is water, grass
and the beaver's splash in the moonless night.

My drumbeat sends
the smell of cedar skywards,
sparking the prayers we offer to red stars.

Then you,
clutching the earth's sweet fur,
the old world wept completely out of you,

begin to howl.

LAST TIME

Crunch of gravel as I park. Miguel's sandbox dark
with rain. Red bucket. Yellow trike. House lights on,
though it's well past ten in the morning.

Beneath the cries of crows, the patchwork green of
midland farms, their mess of hedgerow and blackberry
twitching with the arguments of hungry birds.

I call your name,

and you come walking, out of the office your Pat built,
the one that used to be the cow-shed, now a room of stone
and glass, always bright, even in the gloom of Irish weather.

Dressed in white, you step as though pushing
through water, feeling your way along the wall to greet me,
smiling—that loose, bright smile of those

who've been touched by God—or cancer. You let me hug you.
Body slight as wind, little nubs of your spine, flagstones
of your shoulder bones lifting your cellophane skin.

In the kitchen, smells of ruined toast and bacon, coffee cups
you will not let me wash, counters heaped with work, piles
of papers sliding. I fill the kettle. Flick the switch. We wait.

In the corner by the lit-up Christmas tree, a load of laundry:
jumble of socks, green and red and orange, your blouse,
Pat's jeans, Miguel's tiny football shirt.

You wash the mugs, bring them to the table. On your face
a smile so tight, I'm scared you'll split right down the mid-line,
the way that buds do when you press them.

And then you turn, and for a moment, seem transparent,
swimming in light, pouring it into the distance
that lies between us.

BURIAL

Carrying the loss of you like a bowl of shards,
I walk to the hills, out to where the stones sing hollow
with the cold, and the cry of the raven could crack a body open.

Under pine-dark branches I sit.
Hawks on the wind, high in the wine-blue sky.
Smell of snow in my nostrils, blades of its light in my eyes.

My grief is a river cutting a swathe through the trees,
where the dark at night, shot with ten thousand stars,
pours down shining.

This is the place I will leave what I know of you.
Your life, that tiny house of time, a jewel in my heart
the color of sapphire burning.

I remember the touch of your hand on mine,
the sound of you rasping your last few words: "I do not
believe in a place where the soul's less thirsty."

Into the stone-still space between the mountains
where the sky cracks open its ice-cold light, I shout
your name, crying out to the emptiness to take you home.

There in that space, no bigger than heaven
or hell, I give myself up to my sorrow, letting the blade
of it cut me, 'til I shine.

VISITING YOUR HUSBAND'S GRAVE
For MM, RIP, 2020

After two weeks of freezing weather, sun,
and suddenly you say, "I want to see him."

We speed along the rod-straight roads,
between the fields' combed soil,

old mansions, new condos, woods of
beech, bare and beautiful,

down the long, curved drive of Afterglow Farm,
and over its humped-back bridge, to where

the grass grows long and lush, and the sky
spreads out, as if there were an ocean up ahead.

You stop the car and gesture: "There,
beneath that beech. There isn't a marker."

I leave you, hands on the wheel, head pressed
close to the windshield, and push my way

through the bowing meadow, rippling and
sshshing beneath the fingers of the wind,

to lean my head against *his* tree, to watch
it sweep its branches over the sapphire sky.

A crow's cry cracks the silence. Flies hum.
The silken grasses turn to silver, then to black.

*

"The gardens are just as he liked them," you say
when I get back, "even after all that weather."

"You miss him," I say, and watch you, carefully,
the space around you bigger now

than ever, empty and guarded, as if you knew
you needed to protect it, as if you knew,

that any moment he could step inside,
and call you to him.

ONE A.M AND THE HOUSE IS QUIET

Wanting the bite of cold, I walk outside,
each blade of grass stiff with the fingers of the moon,
blue stars of Orion, shards in the pelt of night, shattered.

A month ago, under that Cedar, my cat was taken,
swift beak of the owl spreading her neck, birds of all kinds feasting.
Your taking took a decade.

I'm not sure which was worse.

Such a dangerous blade this grief is—
gone for months so you think you're done,
'til one, quite unremarkable night,

as you slip towards sleep, here it comes,
slamming into your chest, a fist, a truck,
your home a sudden cairn,

the hollow bowl of your heart
a stone bell ringing.

LAST MOMENT

In this bare room, in that brown box,
my gran lies quiet, Rosary around her fingers,

like her fingers 'round my hand, when through the city,
by the rusted railings, we'd go walking,

naming the flowers that thrilled her: roses, sweet pea,
white carnation, the candled prayer of the magnolia.

I touch her skin, translucent now, like cellophane or pearls.
I touch her bird-boned body, china in its box, broken.

Around me, people gather, shaking hands and heads.
The priest, who never knew her, reads from his book,

sprinkles water, gestures me to move.
When he tries to close her coffin, I lay my forehead on her cheek,

wind my fingers through her hair, and start my wailing.
Polite is not, how I do grieving.

I KNOW YOU CHOSE TO LEAVE
For Dan, RIP, 2014.

Long-limbed and lithe you were, skinless, peeled,
lovely as the leaves of eucalyptus that I used to love,

lovely as the plum I'm holding now, between my fingers,
squeezing its sweetness into the soil that holds you.

When day becomes night,
I go to the tree that helped you leave.

Your memory a lariat
around my heart, squeezing.

Your life, a young branch
leaping into Spring, never to fruit,

its unlived leaves spilling like berries
from my palm, their sweet juice feeding the earth.

I, who thought I could shelter you,
begging you now, to shelter me.

AS YOU LIE DYING FAR AWAY
For Pat, RIP, 2014

In a home, a continent, an ocean, away from you,
I listen for your voice, white flowers of my mind wide open,
your scent like bitter jasmine, haunting me.

I see you, curled like paper in a fire,
thin as the Live Oak leaf that drifted to my feet today,
dried out, but brilliant still, in all its hidden places.

Outside my window, the night, with its crowd
of stars, its blood-dark trees veined against the sky,
fills suddenly with the shuddering owl.

Are you dreaming? Are you flicking
the bright-inked leaves of your days through your fingers,
one last time before the final shuffle?

I remember the rain-filled day by the ocean,
when you took the sea into your hands, spun spume, lace white,
blew it into the palms of my despair.

In that world of grey, you walked in red,
red dress, red shoes, red lips. Your diamante smile
sowing words in me that wove forbidden wings.

Knowing what the old ones say,
when the owl calls out a name,
I cry to you.

Not yet… Not yet.
I want to feel your skin on mine,
one last time.

SINGING OVER THE BONES

When you too are gone, and again I am alone,
I will sit naked, wild, cross-legged on the ground,
And over all the bones I have collected, I will sing alone.

From the forest floor, I will watch the seasons come and go,
Watch the sun and clouds play tag, the earth move 'round,
When you too are gone, and again I am alone.

I will let my nails grow dirty, let my hair grow long.
Let my gaze become a stare, a frown,
And over all the bones I have collected, I will sing alone.

Until the skin begins to glow, firm and creamy,
'Til the flesh begins to grow, until I hear my own
sweet sound, when you too are gone, and again I am alone.

Cupping my hands, I'll hold what I have known,
Daring for as long as needed, to stay down, and
Over all the bones I have collected, I will sing alone.

Until the heart decides no more to be a stone,
And spilling through wild woods, afraid of nothing, it will bound
Once more to hunt, to feed, to howl…

When you too are gone, and again I am alone.

Cris Mulvey was born and raised in Ireland in 1957. She spent the first half of her life as an educator, activist and community organizer, working primarily with low-income women.

At the age of forty, drawn by the beauty of wild nature and by its power to feed, heal and inspire, she moved alone to Montana. There she spent time cavorting with bison, wolves, grizzly bears and wild places and also began to write poetry, short stories, memoir and a novel. She now lives in the foothills of the Sierra Nevada in Northern California, with her husband, Jack, her dog and her two cats, exulting in the company of tall trees, year-round flowers and the rushing majesty of the Yuba river.

She has studied with Marie Howe, Jane Hirshfield, Joe Millar, Dorianne Laux and Ellen Bass. She is the author of the memoir *Mine To Carry: An Irishwoman's Journey Through Forbidden Pregnancy*, published in 2019, and the novel *A Dream of Flying*, yet to be published. Her poems have appeared in a number of literary journals, including the NAUGATUK RIVER REVIEW, the WHITEFISH REVIEW, MOBIUS, LAST NIGHT and the online Poetry Journal WOMEN'S VOICES FOR CHANGE.

www.ingramcontent.com/pod-product-compliance
Lightning Source LLC
LaVergne TN
LVHW041513070426
835507LV00012B/1549